Romantic Poetry

—

Poetry for the Love of Your Life

Romantic Poetry

Poetry for the Love
of Your Life

C. JOSEPH WINTERLE

CJW Press

Copyright © 2023 C. Joseph Winterle

All rights reserved. No part or any portion of this book may be reproduced in any form, mechanical, or digital, or transmitted without the prior written permission of the author, except for the use of brief quotations in a book review.

Cover image: Shutterstock

Cover and interior design by The Book Cover Whisperer:
OpenBookDesign.biz

979-8-9883147-0-7 Hardcover
979-8-9883147-1-4 eBook

FIRST EDITION

CONTENTS

Today 1

Is It Real 3

I Absolutely Can't 5

Wishing I Was Seeing You Today 7

It Just Gets Better 9

The Dream 11

Everything Is Better When We're Together 13

All I Can Do Is Keep Lovin' You 15

Beautiful Love 17

One Hundred Attributes of the Woman I Love 19

In An Instant 27

The Path(s) of Life 29

Going Through the Motions of Life 31

You Never Know 33

Where Is Home 35

There's Something About You 37

You Are 39

My Friend, My Love, My Life 41

I Love ... Our Love 43

That's Why They Call It Love 45

Enthusiasm 47

About the Author 49

*A collection of romantic poems to
inspire and help you express the
love that's in your heart for
your special love . . .*

Today

Thought about you all day today

This day was different from the rest
Why...not sure...but not the best

Thought about you all day today

What I want...may never be
Total disappointment...possibly

Thought about you all day today

There's a better way to think of this
Don't bemoan the longed-for kiss

Thought about you all day today

Focus intently on my special friend
Be happy and positive...the heart will mend

Thought about you all day today

Is It Real

You see the beautiful person, you think it's real
They may be right for you, the real deal

But as the relationship grows a bit
You start to realize, it's not a good fit

You hang on far too long though
Thinking and hoping that love will grow

But soon you realize you must give up
It should be much easier from the very start

You then keep looking and trying too much
They say you should meet such and such

The one that's for real, may be right in your sphere
When you figure it out, you'll try hard to stay near

You hope beyond hope, their feeling is the same
Something that's real, both hearts totally aflame

Is it real

When the sun, the moon and the stars align
Then you'll know that it's very, very fine

I Absolutely Can't

I can't think of anyone more friendly

I can't think of anyone more considerate

I can't think of anyone more warm

I can't think of anyone more interesting

I can't think of anyone more confident

I can't think of anyone more successful

I can't think of anyone more professional

I can't think of anyone more intelligent

I can't think of anyone more caring

I can't think of anyone more invigorating

I can't think of anyone more motivating

I can't think of anyone more perceptive

I can't think of anyone more inspiring

I can't think of anyone more dependable

I can't think of anyone more appealing

I can't think of anyone more beautiful

I can't think of anyone more desirable

I can't think of anyone more special than you

I can't think of anyone more perfect for me than you

I absolutely can't

Wishing I Was Seeing You Today

A day often starts in a simple way

A perfectly normal one as many would say

But there's a special feel in my heart at play

Wishing I was seeing you today

This could be as simple as awaking from sleep

Or possibly thought of as complex and deep

Today's challenges may seem to be steep

They'll be easy, if thoughts of her I'm able to keep

What is it about her, thoughts warm as the sun's ray

Wishing I was seeing you today

What is it about her, that makes me sing like a blue jay

Wishing I was seeing you today

Life without her, those fears she will allay

If in fact, she feels the exact same way

To the one that's so special

Wishing I was seeing you today

It Just Gets Better

Early on, the initial love is strong
She is so beautiful, she can do no wrong

In the flurry of fun, logic is shrouded
Many wonderful thoughts, the brain is clouded

Often then, the excitement may wane
But still progressing down lover's lane

It is normal to adjust to a comfortable pace
Totally in love, but the heart may not race

Sometimes it's different, although very rare
A love so special, an amazing feeling in the air

The days fly by, the love does not slip
Just the sight of her, the heart will still skip

Always thinking of ways to be together
The love is so special, the bond an unbreakable tether

You feel so fortunate, so happy you met her
The love is so perfect, it just gets better

The Dream

Sometimes the thoughtful, wonderful, beautiful,
Romantic, totally amazing woman
Is just a dream

You may spend the rest of your life
Hoping to find her
And you never do

Rarely, rarely, rarely
You actually find love with
The MOST thoughtful, wonderful, beautiful
Romantic, totally amazing woman
You could never imagine

The dream has come true
The dream is YOU

I love you

Everything Is Better When We're Together

The beautiful feeling is always there
Not often noticed, like the smell of fresh air

Normal times are like a special dance
Not even realized, as if in a trance

In more special times, a feeling in the heart
So amazing, so perfect, impossible to part

But it's not hard to determine why
The special love shared, lifts to the sky

Every day is like a beautiful floating feather because
Everything is better when we're together

Post Scriptum
Inspiration comes when not often expected
My love, you are the true inspiration
It flows from you effortlessly
You provide me inspiration and
Total happiness every day of my life

All I Can Do Is Keep Lovin' You

There are important things I wish were better for us
To be with you forever would be my dream, a tremendous plus

But while I long for us to be one, not two
All I can do is keep lovin' you

Your love is all that I really need
I want much more, but life does impede

Your love is all that I want, so true
All I can do is keep lovin' you

Maybe some day, life will improve
You and me...could create a beautiful groove

Maybe some day, life will improve
All I can do is keep lovin' you

So for life, together, we press through
All I can do is keep lovin' you

My love, no one will ever love me like you
For you, I may have to wait forever

But while I wait, I'll be happy, not blue
All I can do is keep lovin' you

You are my love, forever only you
All I can do is keep lovin' you

I love you now
I will love you forever

Beautiful Love

A magical beginning, we know never ending
Excitement each day, a gift we keep sending

A love so wonderful and oh so rare
Perpetual happy thoughts fill the air

Life's challenges sometimes seem unfair
You're sad, then turn, your love is there

Fear can envelop you, even despair
But then you turn, your love is there

Hope abounds, your shared love is sound
Your heart is thrilled, when your love is around

A life with your love, so perfect it would be
But often that perfect life, is only a dream

What you do have, puts you nearly there
A love so beautiful, and oh so rare

One Hundred Attributes of the Woman I Love

Wonderful

Amazing

Beautiful

Thoughtful

Caring

Intelligent

Insightful

Loving

Lovable

Sensitive

Decisive

Appealing

Attractive

Exciting

Sensual

Confident

Heartwarming

Sexy

Enveloping

Seductive

Supportive

Smart

Fit

Hopeful

Friendly

Captivating

Romantic

Conciliatory

Cooperative

Helpful

Honest

Trustworthy

Hard working

Managerial

Talented

Dependable

Encouraging

Energetic

Personable

Approachable

Kind

Generous

Resourceful

Genuine

Problem solver

Realistic

Optimistic

Dreamy

Dreamer

Understanding

Articulate

Successful

High achiever

Warm

Cuddly

Dancer

Witty

Organized

Coordinator

Balanced

Stable

Reliable

Desirable

Traditional

Faith oriented

Willing

Adventurous

Carefree

Prudent

Serious

Wise

Judicious

Innovative

Strong willed

Fun loving

Spirited

Calm

Deliberate

Ingenious

Incredible

Imaginative

Trusting

Distinctive

Classy

Fair

Accountable

Quick thinker

Impressive

Thankful

Happy

Determined

Admired

Respected

Concise

Efficient

Attentive

Loyal

Appreciative

Appreciated

Interesting

It was not difficult to quickly think of one hundred

Attributes to describe you!! The reason it was so easy

For me to describe you, the woman I totally and

Completely love, is attribute number

One Hundred One

Perfect!!!!

You are absolutely perfect in my eyes

And you are absolutely perfect for me!!

I am so incredibly happy for

The love we share

In An Instant

It only took an instant
It only took a smile

To realize what happened
Did not take a long while

It hit me hard, the heart beat faster
It was impossible to look past her

The spark was there months before
I found myself wanting to be near her more

And it was so very wonderful
I fell in love, she was so beautiful

The months and even years flew by
Every day with her was an incredible high

Her beauty I thought could never be surpassed
Wrong, every time, she's more beautiful than the last

But the best and most important of all
One thing certain since the hard fall

I now love her more than ever
My love for her is forever

The Path(s) of Life

How will your life grow
It would be so nice to know
As we progress on our way
It's hard for you to say

To find the right one
As you walk your separate paths
Incredibly low odds
Attributable to high level math

Some think it's just luck
Some think that it's fate
You may or may not
Find the ideal mate

If it happens to you
No longer blue
If it happens to you
The spark of love so true

If it happens to you
Don't try to explain
It may be as simple
As sun following rain

Just a few steps after the smile
What follows will be the quickest mile
No need to prepare
There's a hidden romantic flair

Your separate paths had sorrow
Your separate paths had pain
But it soon will be replaced
Just like a cleansing rain

Your separate paths were happy
Your separate paths content
Now you anticipate this one path
Because it's filled with excitement

The path (s) of life
Merging together
Our beautiful path
Beautiful forever

Going Through the Motions of Life

Life can often turn on a dime
Unexpected...just may be your time

It may be a joy you've never had
Or possibly something that is so sad

It's rarely both in combination
On the tracks of life, but not your station

A beautiful love, tremendous happiness abounds
When you realize it can't be, a deafening sound

You'd jump off gladly
Wishing this love was your station
You don't, oh so sadly
The only hope...reincarnation

The most beautiful love you could ever dream for
Now a beautiful love you can only long for

Now a shattered heart so rife
Going through the motions of life

Never End So Bleak, So Wisely Said
With Perseverance, Better days May Be Ahead

You Never Know

You never know what lies ahead
On a wonderful path you may be led

But you know, in life, it's up to you
Move forward knowing, to yourself be true

You never know where life may lead
Years of hard work, retirement reward, now freed

With the woman you love, will you be able to
Have many happy years, as you so want to do

She is the rare love, not many will ever have
So wonderful, she fills life's proverbial carafe

She's not a dream, she's beautifully real
You think of no other, she's so ideal

She's so everything, she sends you reeling
She wraps your heart in a perfect feeling

The love you share, you know it's forever
The path you seek, such a hopeful endeavor

You never know what lies ahead
On a wonderful path, you both...may be led

Be happy, be true, she's the one for you
And, as life will flow, you never know

Where Is Home

It doesn't matter where we are
It could be near, it could be far

If I'm with you, my heart's never alone
If I'm with you, it's beautifully...home

It could be large, it could be small
It really doesn't matter at all

What matters is our love
A special gift from above

What matters is being with you
Every day, love wonderfully anew

Wherever you are, is where I want to be
Because you're the woman I love, you see

Where is home
Home...so easy to see
Home...with you I want to be
Home...where our love firmly resides
Home...where I'm lucky to be by your side

There's Something About You

I always thought you're wonderful, I love you so
I thought I knew, but it's more, I now know

A love so beautiful, better it could never be
Until I realized, you are perfect for me

There's something about you

I was so happy to be able to say
I am loved in an amazingly special way

I thought a love so deep, but then it grew
I thought a love so deep, but then it sprang anew

There's something about you, my love

I always thought, how wonderful to just be with you
Now, I can't imagine a life without you

There's something about you, my love

We can now conclude, it's a beautiful love, thankfully
We'll be forever in love, it's our destiny

Some look forever for the ideal mate

There's something about you, my love
I'm so happy for us, we always believed in fate

Our special love, so incredibly rare
Our beautiful love, forever we'll share

My love, there's something about you

You Are

You are the bright shining light in my life

You are the reason my heart beats strong
You are the one for whom I always long

You are the shining light, for me so bright
You are the shining light, every day, every night

You are the reason I always smile
It started so quickly, maybe just for a while

You are the reason my face filled with smiles
Now, walking together, a lifetime of happy miles

You are the reason my heart has such flair
Your love is complete with thoughtful loving care

In my being, a love constantly beaming
I see you, so beautiful, perpetual sunshine streaming

Forever and ever, you are the one
Forever and ever, until my life is done

You are the bright shining light in my life

You are

My Friend, My Love, My Life

She captured my heart, never will I part
A love so deep, forever a love to keep
A love so sound, pure happiness abounds

My friend, my love, my life

A special love we willingly share
A beautiful lasting love, one so rare

Absolutely everything to me, she quickly became
Total joy when I knew, for her I was the same

My friend, my love, my life

The key to her heart, I'll try every day
To love her even more, than words can ever say

She is wonderfully perfect for me
Perfect for her, I will always try to be

Her beauty to me, a forever incredible flow
Just being with her, a forever inner glow

My friend, my love, my life
A perfect dream, someday my wife

I Love . . . Our Love

Any love, if it's so true
Is wonderful, if for you

Every love, for the lucky two
Is so very special, for both of you

Many a love, as some may say
Is certainly normal, just in their own way

But when it's your love, a very beautiful one
You peacefully celebrate, when every day is done

You see ... I love ... our love

Ours is the one, that simply keeps growing
The warmth, the joy of our love, always flowing

Nearly impossible to ever describe
Not thinking, you subconsciously imbibe

You cherish the love you always receive
You share your love, so wonderfully hard to conceive

You see ... I love ... our love

The love we share is so incredibly deep
One so rare, you do everything to keep

You give love, you receive love, you share love
You never could dream of such a beautiful love
Never take for granted, this amazing love

I love ... our love

That's Why They Call It Love

It cannot be explained
Trying to, will just leave us drained

There was no warning
As simple as a sun-filled morning

Your beautiful smile, so memorable, an
unexpected exciting start
That moment, so memorable, now a
fixture in my heart

Our incredible love has grown and grown
Fully blossomed and deep, from the seed then sown

You have become my reason for living
Your thoughtful love, perpetually giving

I try every day, to be the one
The one who's your love, until my days are done

What we share is so wonderful
A gift from above

What we share is so wonderful
That's why they call it love

Enthusiasm

Its value is more important than most realize
Since it's a subtle boost to the day like the
sun on the rise

It is something that should be aggressively spread
So the recipient ultimately decides it's from
their own head

With two willing people, even if apart
It creates a tremendously warm
feeling in the heart

If practiced together
It can serve as a tether

It can become a great ploy
To help instill unbridled joy

It can help fill life's pages
And very simply, yes it is contagious

About the Author

JOSEPH GREW UP as part of a large family in a small midwestern city. After earning his undergrad and graduate degrees in the business field, he had a long successful career in financial services. Joseph had a goal to write a collection of poems that would hopefully have a wide appeal. This book is the culmination of that multi-year effort.

About the Author

JOSEPH GREW UP as part of a large family in a small midwestern city. After earning his undergrad and graduate degrees in the business field, he had a long successful career in financial services. Joseph had a goal to write a collection of poems that would hopefully have a wide appeal. This book is the culmination of that multi-year effort.

www.ingramcontent.com/pod-product-compliance
Lightning Source LLC
Chambersburg PA
CBHW020656060526
44119CB00090B/396/J